If I Could Mend Your Heart...

a gift to you:

_____

from:

_____

If I Could Mend Your Heart...

a gift to you:

_____

from:

_____

If I could
mend your heart...

I would weave together
the ragged edges
of your threadbare heart

and soothe your pain
your shock
and disbelief.

composed

I would invite you to
        touch your sorrow
   and feel your feelings

and not pretend to be strong
                or capable
    or composed.

I would listen to all that is u

listen

I would listen,
> without comment,
> to all that is unsettled
>> in your soul

your **doubts**
> your **anger**
> your **fears**
>> about the future.

I would heed your cries
            and probing questions

What might you have done wrong
    or,
        what you might not
                    have done at all.

at all

For more than a single ending,
　　your loss may spark
　　　　　other sorrows
　　other conclusions

　　　　good-byes
and
　　　　thorny adjustments

in every corner of your soul.

If I could mend
your heart...

I would promise not to say,

"*Look how well you're handling things,*"

or,

"*Cheer up,*
God wouldn't give you
more than you could handle,"

or,

"*You'll be over this soon.*"

whisper

Instead, I would whisper in your ear,

"*We live in a fragile and imperfect world*
tinged by brokenness
and cloaked in
unanswered questions.

Some things truly aren't fair.

This is hard."

I would tell you

"Getting over it" *isn't very helpful*

and would ask,

"Can you try to let go of that idea?"

Why
Why
Why
Why

For I don't think loss is about
                    "handling things well,"
            or
    "keeping it all together."

    But about keeping afloat
        in a rising tide of doubt

    Asking the silence,

                    "Why?"

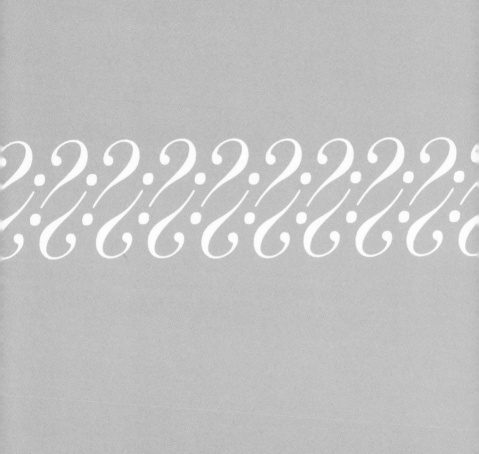

"What is the meaning of this?"

It's about learning to co-exist with
an unwanted visitor,
with alien thoughts,
and depleted spirits.

If I could mend
your heart...

I would draw you a plan and perfect map
to light your path from
confusion and despair,
to
a place of new tomorrows
and rewarding journeys.

release
where anger could release its

A place where anger could

release

its grip on understanding,

and anxiousness

might speak to acceptance.

through prisms of sunlight

I would
shape for you
a fresh way
of seeing,
through prisms
of sunlight,

that warm
your emptiness
and guide the
way to a new
adventure.

Prisms of **sunlight** that temper

your pain with compassion

and replace your doubts with faith,

your grief with **gratitude,**

your fear with **trust.**

compassion

If I could mend

mend

your heart...

I would open wide the doors of renewed hope·
— a hope much larger than wishes.

One that waits

patiently,

willingly,

expectantly,

anticipating future good and
knowing that life is worth living
after all.

This hope that I wish for you
would predict no answers
but invite you
to live the questions.

to live the questions

forward
even in the face of unease

It would not demand exact outcomes
        but ask you to risk letting go
and bid you to move
                forward,
                        even in the
        face of unease.

This fresh hope I send would
    let you step up with courage
                    to the new day

    trusting that even pain
        can be
                transformed.

If I could mend your heart...

mend

I would lead you by the hand
to this place of healing

so that you might once again
walk your own path
and make memories.

I would share with you a secret

Joy

"Joy is not about

                                   music

             and

                                 dance

                                           and

                                 laughter,

                                      but about

the acceptance of Life.

Healing

Healing happens only where
fear and love,
joy and sorrow,
tears and smiles,
can forge a
lasting peace.

Joy

The healing I speak of lies
not in some safe place along the way,
but in
having made
the journey

stage

by

stage.

Until you reach that place,
a place
you may not now believe
exists,

your space

I will save your space

and watch with confidence

for your smiles yet to be.

Mary Farr is a writer, teacher and pastoral counselor of adult and pediatric patients, of families of seriously ill children, and has worked with medical staffs dealing with crisis. Mary is a frequent presenter at conferences and seminars related to health and wholeness. She is the mother of two and a resident of St. Paul, MN.

copyright © 2001 Mary I. Farr

ISBN 0-916773-91-4
ISBN 13: 978-0916773-915

design and production by
Pettit Network, Inc., Afton, MN 55001

To order a single copy or for resale copies, contact,
  BOOK PEDDLERS
  2828 Hedberg Drive
  Minnetonka, MN 55305
  952-912-0036 • fax: -0105
  www.bookpeddlers.com

      printed in China
  06 07 08 09   8 7 6 5 4